MIGHTY MACHINES IN ACTION

Pickup Trucks

by Chris Bowman

BELLWETHER MEDIA • MINNEAPOLIS, MN

Note to Librarians, Teachers, and Parents:

Blastoff! Readers are carefully developed by literacy experts and combine standards-based content with developmentally appropriate text.

Level 1 provides the most support through repetition of high-frequency words, light text, predictable sentence patterns, and strong visual support.

Level 2 offers early readers a bit more challenge through varied simple sentences, increased text load, and less repetition of high-frequency words.

Level 3 advances early-fluent readers toward fluency through increased text and concept load, less reliance on visuals, longer sentences, and more literary language.

Level 4 builds reading stamina by providing more text per page, increased use of punctuation, greater variation in sentence patterns, and increasingly challenging vocabulary.

Level 5 encourages children to move from "learning to read" to "reading to learn" by providing even more text, varied writing styles, and less familiar topics.

Whichever book is right for your reader, Blastoff! Readers are the perfect books to build confidence and encourage a love of reading that will last a lifetime!

This edition first published in 2018 by Bellwether Media, Inc.

No part of this publication may be reproduced in whole or in part without written permission of the publisher. For information regarding permission, write to Bellwether Media, Inc., Attention: Permissions Department, 5357 Penn Avenue South, Minneapolis, MN 55419.

Library of Congress Cataloging-in-Publication Data
Names: Bowman, Chris, 1990- author.
Title: Pickup Trucks / by Chris Bowman.
Description: Minneapolis, MN : Bellwether Media, Inc., 2018. | Series: Blastoff! Readers: Mighty Machines in Action | Includes bibliographical references and index. | Audience: Ages 5-8. | Audience: K to Grade 3.
Identifiers: LCCN 2017031304 (print) | LCCN 2017035633 (ebook) | ISBN 9781626177574 (hardcover : alk. paper) | ISBN 9781681034621 (ebook)
Subjects: LCSH: Pickup trucks–Juvenile literature.
Classification: LCC TL230.5.P49 (ebook) | LCC TL230.5.P49 B69 2018 (print) | DDC 629.223/2–dc23
LC record available at https://lccn.loc.gov/2017031304

Editor: Rebecca Sabelko   Designer: Tamara JM Peterson

Printed in the United States of America, North Mankato, MN.

Table of Contents

A Day's Work — 4

Many Uses — 8

Engines, Cabs, and Beds — 12

Keep on Trucking — 20

Glossary — 22

To Learn More — 23

Index — 24

A DAY'S WORK

A man pulls a pickup truck up to a building. He loads wood into the truck's **bed**.

bed

Then he **hauls** it to
a **construction site**.

Later, the man gets ready for a weekend of fishing. He hooks his boat to the truck and drives to the lake.

The pickup truck helps the
man complete many tasks!

MANY USES

Pickup trucks are found anywhere there are roads.

MACHINE PROFILE
2017 FORD F-150 XLT

engine: 3.5L Ti-VCT V6 engine
transmission: 6-speed
length: 19 feet (5.8 meters)
height: 6 feet (1.8 meters)
width (with mirrors): 8 feet (2.4 meters)

trailer

Many work on farms and job sites to carry heavy loads. They often tow big **trailers**.

Some drivers have pickups
for everyday use.

Large pickup trucks have room to drive families around. There is also space to carry items from shopping trips.

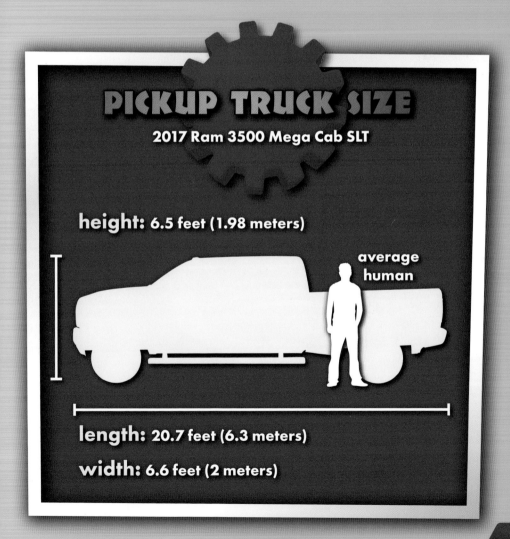

PICKUP TRUCK SIZE

2017 Ram 3500 Mega Cab SLT

height: 6.5 feet (1.98 meters)

average human

length: 20.7 feet (6.3 meters)

width: 6.6 feet (2 meters)

ENGINES, CABS, AND BEDS

Many pickups are powerful vehicles. Some have **four-wheel drive** or **diesel engines**.

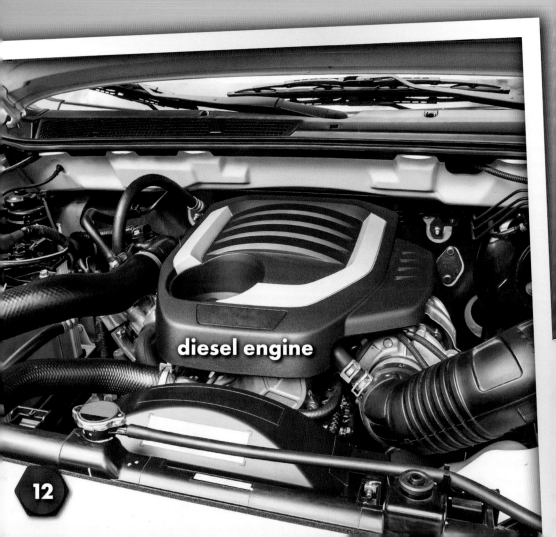

diesel engine

plow

These allow trucks to push **plows** and pull heavy **cargo**.

Drivers and passengers sit in the **cab**. These often have two doors.

cab

back door

Some cabs have back doors that open to a second row of seats.

Truck beds can be different sizes. They are often loaded up with work supplies.

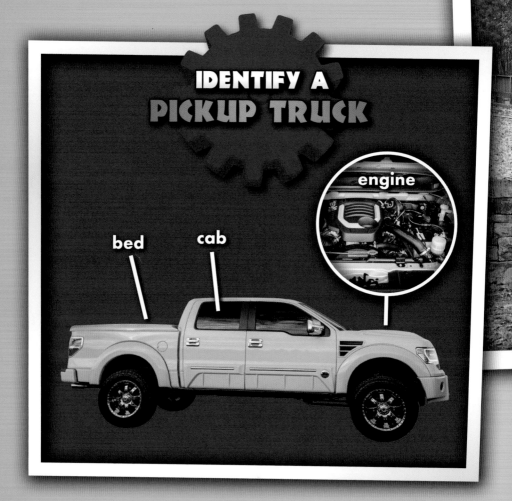

IDENTIFY A
PICKUP TRUCK

engine

bed   cab

They can also carry supplies
for fun. Sometimes, trucks
have campers on their beds!

Most pickup trucks
have four wheels.

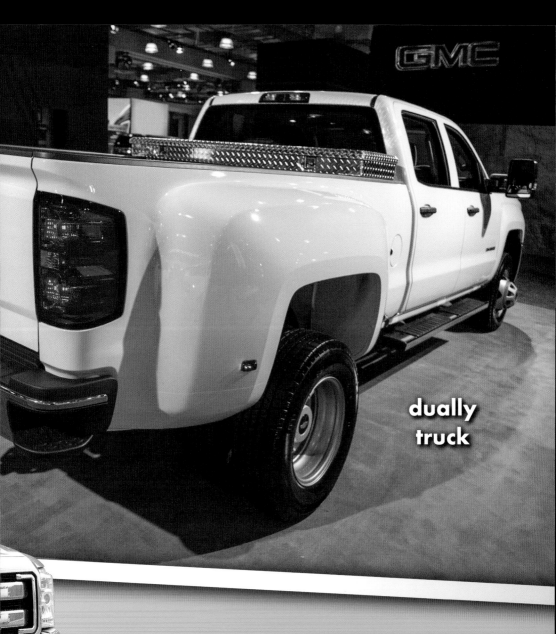

dually
truck

Dually trucks have six. The extra wheels help them tow heavier loads.

19

Pickup trucks were first built to make jobs easier. But they have become common for everyday driving.

Whether carrying wood or pulling a boat, there is a pickup truck for every use!

Glossary

bed—the flat surface behind the cab used to carry objects

cab—the part of the pickup truck where the driver and passengers sit

cargo—something that is carried by a pickup truck

construction site—a place where something is built

diesel engines—loud engines that burn diesel fuel and are often used in big machines

dually—a pickup truck with two extra wheels at the rear

four-wheel drive—a system that allows pickups to power all four wheels

hauls—carries

plows—blades used to push snow or dirt

trailers—long platforms or boxes with wheels that are pulled behind pickup trucks

To Learn More

AT THE LIBRARY

Bowman, Chris. *Monster Trucks*. Minneapolis, Minn.: Bellwether Media, 2017.

Riggs, Kate. *Pickup Trucks*. Mankato, Minn.: Creative Education, 2017.

Schuh, Mari. *Trucks*. North Mankato, Minn.: Capstone Press, 2017.

ON THE WEB

Learning more about pickup trucks is as easy as 1, 2, 3.

1. Go to www.factsurfer.com.

2. Enter "pickup trucks" into the search box.

3. Click the "Surf" button and you will see a list of related web sites.

With factsurfer.com, finding more information is just a click away.

Index

bed, 4, 16, 17

cab, 14, 15, 16

campers, 17

cargo, 13

construction site, 5

doors, 14, 15

drivers, 10, 14

dually, 19

engines, 8, 12, 16

farms, 9

four-wheel drive, 12

hauls, 5

loads, 4, 9, 16, 19

passengers, 14

plows, 13

roads, 8

seats, 15

size, 8, 11, 16

supplies, 16, 17

trailers, 9

uses, 7, 9, 10, 11, 13, 20, 21

wheels, 18, 19

The images in this book are reproduced through the courtesy of: Ford Motor Company, front cover (truck), pp. 6-7; saranya33, front cover (sky); LovePHY, pp. 4-5 (background); ltdedigos, pp. 4-5 (truck); DreamPictures/ Getty Images, p. 5; Darren Brode, p. 8; Maxwell De Araujo Rodrigues, p. 9; Monkey Business Images, p. 10; sommai damrongpanich, p. 12; robert cicchetti, p. 13; Art Konovalov, pp. 14, 15, 18; Kyle Brutke, p. 16 (truck); Prisma by Dukas Presseagentur GmbH/ Alamy, p. 17; Wachira W, p. 16 (engine); Ed Aldridge, p. 19; Anne Kitzman, pp. 20-21.